AL
BIOS

# SELENA GOMEZ

## By Marie Morreale

**Children's Press**®
An Imprint of Scholastic Inc.

Photos ©: cover: Tom Donoghue/Polaris/Newscom; back cover: Joey Terrill Photography; 1: Tom Donoghue/Polaris/Newscom; 2-3: Mat Hayward/Getty Images; 4-5: Mike Coppola/Getty Images; 6-7: Joey Terrill Photography; 7: Leopix / Splash News/Newscom; 8: Michael Tran/Getty Images; 9: Hit Entertainment/Everett Collection; 10: K Mazur/TCA 2008/Getty Images; 11: Jeff Daly/ Getty Images; 12: Larry Busacca/Getty Images; 13 top right: Brian Ach/Getty Images; 13 top left: farha/Shutterstock, Inc.; 13 center: Michael Kraus/Shutterstock, Inc.; 13 bottom left: Kevin Mazur/ Getty Images; 13 bottom right: s_bukley/Shutterstock, Inc.; 14: Michael Simon/Startraks Photo; 15 top: Dragoneye/Dreamstime; 15 center: Michael Tran/Getty Images; 15 bottom: M.G.M/ Superstock, Inc.; 16: Disney/Splash News/Newscom; 18 top: Victor Chavez/Getty Images; 18 bottom: John Shearer/TCA 2009/Getty Images; 19 top: Brian Ach/Getty Images; 19 bottom: Vallery Jean/ Getty Images; 20: Fox 2000 Pictures/Everett Collection; 21 top: Twentieth Century Fox Film Corporation/Everett Collection; 21 bottom: Theo Wargo/Getty Images; 22 top: Fox 2000 Pictures/ Everett Collection; 22 bottom: MU1 WENN Photos/Newscom; 23: Richard Isaac/ZUMA Press/Newscom; 25 left: Lisa Lake/Stringer/ Getty Images; 25 right: PacificCoastNews/Newscom; 26: Steve Jennings/Stringer/Getty Images; 27: FS2 WENN Photos/Newscom; 28: Brian Rasic/Rex USA; 30: Michael Simon/Startraks Photo; 31: Kevin Winter/Getty Images; 33: Mat Hayward/Getty Images; 34: Michael Simon/Startraks Photo; 35: Derek Storm/Splash News/ Newscom; 36 main: Larry Busacca/Getty Images; 36 background and throughout: conejota/Thinkstock; 37: infukyo-01/INFphoto. com/Newscom; 37 paper texture background and throughout: Nonnakrit/Shutterstock, Inc.; 38 top: Helga Esteb/Shutterstock, Inc., 38 center, 38 bottom: DFree/Shutterstock, Inc.; 39 top: Helga Esteb/Shutterstock, Inc.; 39 center: Tinseltown/Shutterstock, Inc.; 39 bottom: Helga Esteb/Shutterstock, Inc.; 40 top right: Barnsley, Dome, PacificCoastNews/Newscom; 40 top left: Mariusz Blach/ Dreamstime; 40 bottom left: Elkeflorida/Dreamstime; 40 bottom right: sarsmis/Shutterstock, Inc.; 41 Elton John: Brian Rasic/ Rex USA; 41 crayon: Lucie Lang/Shutterstock, Inc.; 41 notebook paper background: My Life Graphic/Shutterstock, Inc.; 41 pushpin: seregam/Thinkstock; 42: Mark Sullivan/Getty Images; 45: infusla-53/INFphoto.com/Newscom.

Library of Congress Cataloging-in-Publication Data J791.4
Morreale, Marie.                                  MOR
 Selena Gomez / by Marie Morreale.
  pages cm. — (Real bios)
 Includes bibliographical references and index.
 ISBN 978-0-531-21571-5 (library binding) — ISBN 978-0-531-21663-7 (pbk.)
 1. Gomez, Selena, 1992– —Juvenile literature. 2. Actors—United States—Biography—Juvenile literature. 3. Singers—United States—Biography—Juvenile literature. I. Title.
 PN2287.G585M67 2016
 791.4302'8092—dc23 [B]                          2015005369

© 2016 Scholastic Inc.

All rights reserved. Published in 2016 by Children's Press, an imprint of Scholastic Inc.

Printed in the United States 113
SCHOLASTIC, CHILDREN'S PRESS, and associated logos are trademarks and/or registered trademarks of Scholastic Inc.

1 2 3 4 5 6 7 8 9 10 R 25 24 23 22 21 20 19 18 17 16

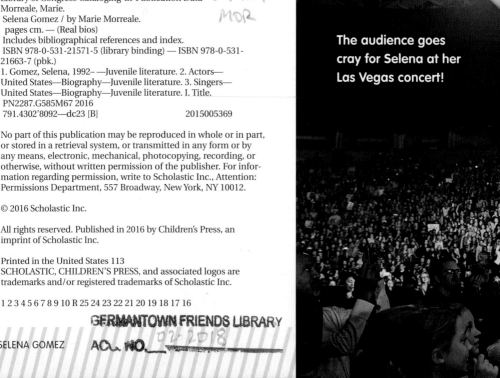

The audience goes cray for Selena at her Las Vegas concert!

# MEET SELENA!

## AMERICA'S SWEETHEART

You first fell in love with Selena Gomez when she was just 15 years old and starring on *Wizards of Waverly Place*. The magic she practiced on the show may have been imaginary, but the spell she cast over millions of fans was real! Not only was *Wizards* the top-rated show on Disney, but when Selena turned her attention to music, she packed concert arenas all over the world. She's won honors ranging from Teen Choice Awards to Nickelodeon's Kids' Choice Awards to MTV Music Video Awards. She was even named *Glamour* magazine's Woman of the Year in 2012!

Awards aren't the only thing motivating Selena to reach new heights, though. She loves what she does, and she connects with each and every one of her fans, the Selenators! And in spite of all the flash that surrounds her, she is still just a typical American girl. In this *Real Bio*, you'll learn a ton of fun facts about Selena. Did you know that her fave snack is a crunchy pickle? That Taylor Swift is her BFF? That she loves horror movies? Read on and get to know the real Selena Gomez!

# CONTENTS

Meet Selena! ................ 3

**CHAPTER ONE**
The Beginning............. 6

**CHAPTER TWO**
Superstar.................. 16

**CHAPTER THREE**
Q&A.......................... 28

**CHAPTER FOUR**
Bits & Pieces................ 36

**CHAPTER FIVE**
What's Next?............... 42

Resources ................. 46
Glossary ................... 46
Index....................... 47
About the Author.......... 48

It was a merry, merry Christmas when Selena performed at Boston's KISS 108's Jingle Ball in 2013.

# A STAR IS BORN

## SELENA'S JOURNEY FROM TEXAS TO HOLLYWOOD

You might be surprised to learn that Selena Gomez was not a born-and-bred child of Hollywood. Believe it or not, her story began a long way from the glitz and glamour of the world's showbiz capital. Born in a suburb of Dallas, Texas, Selena is the only child of Mandy and Ricardo Gomez. She was named after the late singer Selena, who was also from Texas. This means she had a musical role model from the very beginning!

Selena's early childhood wasn't picture-perfect. She was born when her mom was still a teenager, and her parents divorced when she was just five years old. Though both her mom and dad were in her life, it wasn't easy. "My mom gave up everything for me, had three jobs, supported me, sacrificed her life for me," Selena told perezhilton.com.

Selena has been entertaining people her whole life!

**Twitter Stats**
Selena has more than 26 million followers!

In spite of the hard times, Selena and her mom had wonderful times together. Summing up her life back then, Selena told *Elle* magazine, "I can remember about seven times when our car got stuck on the highway because we'd run out of gas money . . . [but my mom] saved up to take me to concerts. She took me to museums and aquariums to teach me about the world, about what's real."

One of Mandy's jobs was at a local community theater, and she often brought Selena along because she couldn't afford a babysitter. This early introduction to acting and singing sparked something in Selena. She

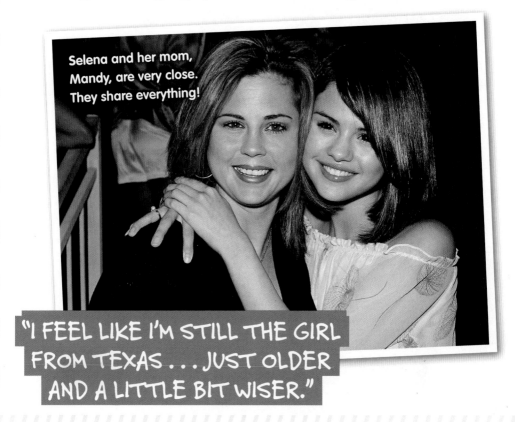

Selena and her mom, Mandy, are very close. They share everything!

"I FEEL LIKE I'M STILL THE GIRL FROM TEXAS . . . JUST OLDER AND A LITTLE BIT WISER."

Selena and her Texas BFF, Demi Lovato, got their start on *Barney & Friends*.

Demi Lovato

Selena Gomez

explained to *Emmy*, "Because I didn't have a brother or sister, I had to entertain myself. I would perform plays and I would sing and I would write stuff."

The urge to perform was growing in Selena. When she was seven years old, her mom took her to an **audition** for the *Barney & Friends* TV series. "It was really hot, and there were 1,400 kids in a line that wrapped around the building three times," Selena told *Elle*. "My mom said we could go home but I wanted to stay." Selena won the role of Gianna, but she remembers being a little overwhelmed. "I was very shy when I was little," she told *People* magazine. "I didn't know what 'camera right' was. I didn't know what **blocking** was. I learned everything from *Barney*."

Selena and Demi recall old memories backstage at the 2008 Teen Choice Awards.

Another gift from *Barney* was the chance to meet fellow Texan Demi Lovato. The two girls auditioned and won roles on the show together, beginning a lifelong friendship.

Selena was in the *Barney* cast from 2001 until 2003. Around that time, she also had small roles in the movies *Spy Kids 3-D: Game Over* and *Walker, Texas Ranger: Trial by Fire.*

Things were happening with Selena's career, but everything wasn't all hearts and flowers in her personal life. Selena went to public school through the eighth grade. Even though she had acting experience, she was still shy. She wasn't part of the popular crowd. "There was a group of girls who were on the meaner side," she told *Tiger Beat.* "It's a big deal trying to fit in at school and making sure you're in the in crowd. . . . Everybody goes through that."

Things changed dramatically for Selena when she was 13. "After *Barney*, I kept working steadily in commercials,

because that's all they really had in Dallas," she told *Time Out New York Kids* magazine. "Then the Disney Channel had a nationwide casting search, so I sent them my tape and two weeks later they flew me to California. It was the first time I'd ever been there."

The Disney Channel was looking for a new crop of kids for its upcoming sitcoms. Selena went to Los Angeles— and so did her BFF Demi Lovato. Selena was very nervous because she knew that a Disney show could be her big break. "My first audition did not go well," Selena told heatworld.com. "I was very awkward. It was in front of a bunch of suits at Disney and I definitely felt I blew it. It took me a long time to let go."

Minnie Mouse welcomes Selena to the 2008 Disney Channel Games at Disney World's Epcot Center.

Well, Selena hardly blew it! Both she and Demi were picked for Disney Channel shows. Selena's first outing for the channel was a guest spot on *The Suite Life of Zack & Cody* in 2006. Then, in 2007, she won the role of Mikayla on Miley Cyrus's hit show, *Hannah Montana*. She also starred in two **pilots** for possible spin-offs of *Suite Life* and *Lizzie McGuire*. Neither was picked up, but third time's the charm. Selena's next role was Alex Russo in *Wizards of Waverly Place*.

Selena costarred in the hit series with David Henrie,

# FACT FILE

## THE BASICS

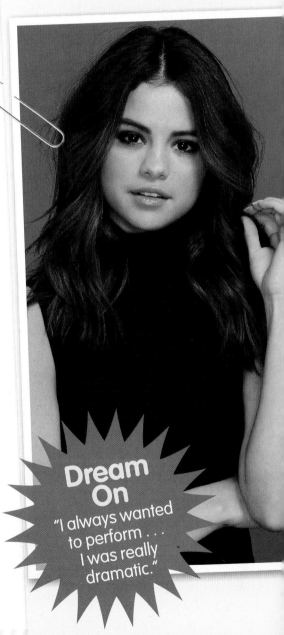

### Dream On

"I always wanted to perform . . . I was really dramatic."

**FULL NAME:** Selena Marie Gomez

**NICKNAME:** Sel

**BIRTHPLACE:** Grande Prairie, Texas

**PARENTS:** Dad Ricardo Joel Gomez, mom Amanda Dawn "Mandy" Teefey, and stepdad Brian Teefey

**SIBLINGS:** Half sisters Gracie Elliot Teefey and Victoria Gomez

**PETS:** Dogs Willie, Baylor, Wallace, Fina, Chazz, and Chip

**MIDDLE SCHOOL:** Danny Jones Middle School

**SIGNATURE CLOTHING LINE:** Dream Out Loud for Kmart

**ROLE MODELS:** Jennifer Lopez, Beyoncé

**HONOR:** UNICEF Ambassador—the youngest ever!

**MOST TICKLISH SPOT:** Her feet

**DREAM:** To invent pickle-flavored chewing gum

**FANS' NICKNAME:** Selenators

**TWITTER FOLLOWERS:** More than 26 million

**WEB SITE:** www.selenagomez.com

Jake T. Austin, Jennifer Stone, and Maria Canals-Barrera from 2007 until 2012. *Wizards* was about a New York City family that led a normal life as restaurant owners but were actually wizards behind the scenes. It quickly became the top show on the Disney Channel.

Selena's Disney days were just the beginning of a career where she rarely heard the word no. By 2012, when *Wizards of Waverly Place* ended its run, Selena was ready to try new things and have new adventures. She was a star on the rise! Ready, willing, and able to soar!

FACT FILE

**FAVORITES**

Selena poses for the cameras at the premiere for *Another Cinderella Story*.

**SCHOOL SUBJECT:** Science

**SPORT:** Basketball

**CARTOON CHARACTER:** Mickey Mouse

**ANIMAL:** Tiger

**SINGERS:** Christina Aguilera, Katy Perry, Britney Spears

**BANDS:** Paramore, Fall Out Boy

**ACTOR:** Johnny Depp

**ACTRESS:** Rachel McAdams

**COLOR:** Green

**HOLIDAY:** Halloween

**BRAND OF JEANS:** J Brand

**RESTAURANT:** Maggiano's Little Italy

**VACATION SPOTS:** Puerto Rico, Hawaii, Paris

**CLOTHING STORES:** Urban Outfitters, American Apparel

**BODY CREAM:** Oil of Olay

**SOCIAL MEDIA:** Instagram

**FILMS:** The Wizard of Oz and Alice in Wonderland

**MOVIE GENRE:** Horror

**ROOM ACCESSORY:** Yankee Candles

## Teen Idol
Selena had a crush on Jesse McCartney when she was a tween!

# Disney Wizards OF WAVERLY PLACE

**Strong**

"I believe in a lot of girl power!"

Selena started her run on *Wizards of Waverly Place* in 2007.

# GIRL POWER

## FROM WIZARD TO TEEN QUEEN!

n May 2011, *Wizards of Waverly Place* taped its final episode. It was the last time the cast and crew would all work together. It was a bittersweet time for Selena. "I just tried to take everything in," she told *GL* magazine about the final day on set. "The whole crew on that show has played a huge part of my life. They all watched me grow up and helped raise me in different ways."

Selena's career was bigger than just *Wizards of Waverly Place*, though. In addition to her other acting roles, she also made her way into the music world with her band Selena Gomez & the Scene. They released three studio albums—*Kiss & Tell* (2009), *A Year Without Rain* (2010), and *When the Sun Goes Down* (2011). The single "Naturally," from *Kiss & Tell*, was a major hit that received a lot of radio play. The singles "Round & Round" and "A Year Without Rain" from *A Year Without Rain* went platinum, which means they sold more than one million copies. Singles "Who Says"

## Home Sweet Home

Selena bought a $3 million estate in Calabasas, California.

Selena earned a gold record award for her album *When the Sun Goes Down.*

and "Love You Like a Love Song" from *When the Sun Goes Down* also went platinum. "Who Says" is still one of Selena's favorite songs. "It's my anthem for girls," she told *Seventeen* magazine. "When I perform it, I have everyone sing with me, and I don't sing. I want them to hear themselves say, 'Who says I'm not perfect? Who says I'm not beautiful? Who says I'm not worth it?' It's the coolest thing for girls to *feel* that."

# Selena's Timeline

## On the Road with Selena!

**2001**
Selena wins the role of Gianna on *Barney & Friends*

**AUGUST 9, 2009**
Selena wins a Teen Choice Award for *Princess Protection Program*

Even while she was achieving huge success with the Scene, Selena wanted to spend more time making movies. She was careful to make the right career choices. In 2008, she turned down a role in the Disney Channel movie *High School Musical 3: Senior Year*. She told the *New York Daily News*, "*High School Musical 3* is cute, and I think it would be a great opportunity for someone else. But I passed on it because I didn't want to do it. I plan to take other roles in acting that are challenging for me."

Selena hugs a fan at the launch of the 2008 UNICEF Trick-or-Treat campaign.

**SEPTEMBER 29, 2009**
Selena Gomez & the Scene's first album, *Kiss & Tell*, is released

**JULY 23, 2010**
*Ramona and Beezus* opens in theaters

**AUGUST 8, 2010**
Selena wins four Teen Choice Awards

Selena was interested in challenging herself, but she still wanted to remain a good role model for her "littles," which is what she calls her younger fans. "I just wouldn't want to do anything that might make them uncomfortable," she told *Teen Vogue*. That's why the 2010 movie *Ramona and Beezus* was a perfect choice for her. "It was my first project that was in theaters," Selena told Scholastic Classroom Magazines. "I'd done DVDs and I'd done television and stuff that I'm comfortable with. This was definitely . . . very hard for me. But in the end I actually learned a lot about movies, about people, and Joey [King] who played my little sister became my sister! She's just so sweet and wonderful!"

"SOME KIDS PLAY SOCCER. ACTING IS MY SPORT."

Playing Beezus was the perfect challenge for Selena—because in real life, she is nothing like her on-screen counterpart. "Beezus [was] really hard for me to get into

**SEPTEMBER 21, 2010**
Selena Gomez & the Scene's second album, *A Year Without Rain*, is released

**JUNE 28, 2011**
Selena Gomez & the Scene's third album, *When the Sun Goes Down*, is released

**JULY 1, 2011**
*Monte Carlo* is released

Selena poses with her *Ramona and Beezus* costar Joey King.

because she's very uncomfortable in her skin and she's just very studious and is always trying to be someone that she's not half the time," she continued with Scholastic. "She [isn't] really carefree and just doesn't let loose."

Her next film was *Monte Carlo*. She played Grace, a normal American teen who is on a Paris vacation with her friends, played by Katie Cassidy and Leighton Meester. In the movie, Selena also plays Cordelia Winthrop Scott, a British heiress whom Grace is

**AUGUST 4, 2011**
Selena wins the Teen Choice Award for TV Actress—Comedy

**DECEMBER 2012**
Selena is named *Glamour* magazine's Woman of the Year

**APRIL 6, 2013**
"Come & Get It" is released

**JULY 23, 2013**
*Stars Dance* is released

(L to R): Leighton Meester, Selena Gomez, and Katie Cassidy star in *Monte Carlo*.

mistaken for. Playing a double role was an entirely new experience for the young actress, but she felt that it was a good career choice. "I feel that *Monte Carlo* is definitely still a teen comedy, which I'm okay with," she explained to CinemaNerdz.com. "It is a little bit older than some of the things that I've done before, but I still feel like my younger generation [of fans] can watch it as well as an older generation . . . I feel like that's in the transition place that I'm in."

**AUGUST 11, 2013**
Selena wins Teen Choice Awards for Female Summer Music Star, Female Hottie, and Break-Up Song ("Come & Get It")

**AUGUST 14, 2013**
The *Stars Dance* tour is launched in Vancouver, Canada

**AUGUST 10, 2014**
Selena wins Teen Choice Awards for Ultimate Choice and Female Hottie

After *Monte Carlo*, Selena made a **cameo** appearance as herself in *The Muppets* and provided the voice of Mavis in *Hotel Transylvania*. By 2013, Selena was ready to move from teen movies to something a little more mature. In 2013, her movies *Aftershock* and *Getaway* hit theaters. She released even more films, including *Hotel Transylvania 2* and *The Revised Fundamentals of Caregiving* in 2015 and 2016.

Though Selena had decided to concentrate on the acting side of her career, she didn't give up on music. By 2012, rumors were buzzing that Selena was back in the recording studio working on her debut solo album. The Scene had disbanded when Selena decided to concentrate on acting, but it was obvious that she was ready to take that next major step in her music career. In April 2013, "Come & Get It," the first single from her new album, *Stars Dance*, was released. It was the biggest hit of Selena's music career so far. The album was released in July 2013.

**NOVEMBER 23, 2014**
Selena performs "The Heart Wants What It Wants" at the 2014 American Music Awards

**SEPTEMBER 25, 2015**
*Hotel Transylvania 2* is released

**2015**
*In Dubious Battle* is released

**2016**
*The Revised Fundamentals of Caregiving* is released

It was Selena's first album to debut at number one on the *Billboard* 200 chart. The *Stars Dance* tour started in August 2013 and finished in November. It took her all over the world. It was an amazing musical geography lesson!

Selena got to work on her second solo album in 2014. She found herself far from the teen world of her earlier career. Cowriting the song "The Heart Wants What It Wants" showed her a new area of growth. "It was a place where I'm going to start a whole new chapter of music," she told Inquisitr.com. "Once I realized that . . . I had something to talk about. . . . If I was 15 years old, what was I talking about love for? . . . It's my 20s. It's supposed to be confusing. That's when I decided that this is a really good time for me to share my heart, where I'm coming from, when I felt like I was being pulled in a million directions. Whether it was publicly or personally, my voice was heard. I'm excited to be able to have my heart into my music now."

As she has become more mature, Selena has also started focusing more on business. In 2010, she launched her Dream Out Loud fashion line for girls. Selena told *MTV News*, "I want the pieces that can be easy to dress up or down, and the fabrics being eco-friendly and organic is super important. . . . Also, the

> EVERY WEEK, SELENA MAKES A DAY FOR HERSELF "TO JUST HANG OUT."

Both Selena's Dream Out Loud line (above left) and her Adidas Neo line (right) scream fun and comfort.

tags will all have some of my inspirational quotes on them. I'm just looking to send a good message."

Selena was very involved in the creation of her personal fragrance, which is named after her. In 2013, she also began working with Adidas to create a fashion line called Neo. When that addition to her work schedule was announced, Selena told Capitalfm.com, "I love playing around with fashion and like clothes that are fun, easy to wear and comfortable. My collection has a rock chic theme and it's confident, rebellious and fun. It's also a little bit darker and I think it encourages girls to put their own stamp on their individuality and show confidence in what they are wearing."

Because of her incredible success, Selena feels like she has a lot to give back—not just to her fans, but also to kids who have never seen *Wizards of Waverly Place*. In 2009, Selena was named a UNICEF Ambassador—she was the youngest person ever picked for the position! Her first mission was to go to Ghana, Africa, to learn about the poverty in many parts of the country. UNICEF has food, health care, environmental, and educational programs all over the world. Selena wanted to use her name to let her fans know about the conditions in a place like Ghana.

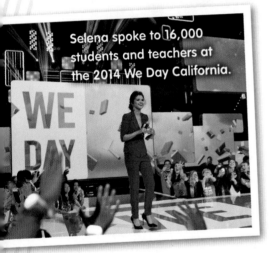
Selena spoke to 16,000 students and teachers at the 2014 We Day California.

In 2014, Selena addressed the audience of the first annual We Day conference. Kids of all ages from all over the United States were in the audience. Urging the kids to help others, she told them, "You are changing the world. Please be kind to each other, and love and inspire people. Let's change the game. …Stay true to yourself and know that we all have each other's back."

Acting, music, fashion, and charity work—these are the many sides of Selena Gomez. But even with such a busy life, she still has time for her friends. It's well known that Selena is very close to fellow superstars Taylor Swift, Demi Lovato, and Emma Stone, and she's still close to her childhood friends back in Texas. "It's good to have both," she told *Harper's Bazaar*. "It's great to just pick up a phone and call Taylor and say, 'I have people following me, and I'm having a bad day,' but if I were to say that to someone else, it's like, 'Oh, boo hoo.' But it's nice to have people back home that grew up with me too."

As for Taylor, Selena admits that she has learned a lot from the award-winning singer. They share their personal and professional positives and negatives, and they totally understand each other. "It's so funny because in so many ways we're the same person that it freaks us out," she told British *Cosmopolitan*. "But then there are other ways where we are so different, where we sort of complement each other. … We just support each other and throughout everything we go through, we know we both understand. … We're always there for each other." What else? Selena is always there for her fans, friends, and family!

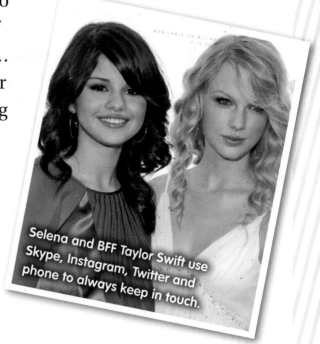

Selena and BFF Taylor Swift use Skype, Instagram, Twitter and phone to always keep in touch.

Hands up in the air!
Selena turns up for
London fans in 2013!

# SELENA SPILLS THE BEANS

## THE MEGA-STAR GOES ONE-ON-ONE WITH YOU!

Selena reveals her thoughts on fashion, being a role model, her red carpet routine, and her love for Mexican food. Get the whole scoop!

**On books that influenced her . . .** "One that made me who I am is *Alice in Wonderland* because I read that book so much growing up. I felt like I was Alice all the time. I felt like I was wandering around, having no idea where I was from or no idea where I was going. I had visions of all these imaginary, crazy things. I liked *The Wizard of Oz* a lot as well. I definitely like all of James Patterson's books. They're really comforting to me."

**On why she keeps a journal . . .** "Sometimes my journals consist of lyrics or quotes. If I read a book and I find a line I like, I'll write it down and quote the book underneath. . . . [Journals are] very therapeutic. . . .

On the set! Selena checks out footage of her "Come & Get It" video with the director.

When you want to get something out and may not feel comfortable talking to your friends or your family and you just kind of want to get it out of you. I think that a journal is your best friend in life. . . . It's like a listening ear that will listen to you and not judge you or anything. It's just kind of there."

**On being a Latina role model . . .** "Growing up, [teen idols] were all blond, with light-colored eyes. I wanted to be that. I didn't realize how important it was to represent my background and my culture until parents of Latin descent started coming up to me. Then it clicked. I can represent a different generation and a different culture."

**On getting-into-performing advice . . .** "The only advice I ever tell people is simple: You have to be passionate about this industry if you want to make it. It's not worth it if you don't really love performing because there are a lot of people who will try and bring you down. . . . There's a lot of rejection in this industry and it's tough. There are also a lot of obstacles that you have to go through and it can really be exhausting. But, if you love it, that's all that matters."

iTUNES #
One
"I Want to Know You" hit the top of the dance charts.

Selena Gomez & the Scene performs at the 2011 Teen Choice Awards.

**On being a famous young actress in Hollywood . . .** "You have this pressure [to fit in] and you want people to like you. I try my best to be a good person and be the best I can be. . . . I feel like everything that I'm doing right now should not be taken too seriously. I should be able to have fun and enjoy where I'm at! So I don't want to spend my time hiding out worrying about all of that."

**On besties . . .** "I've gotten to the point where the label of 'best friend' is so ridiculous. If you have three people in your life that you can trust, you can consider yourself the luckiest person in the whole world. I have a lot of wonderful people in my life—probably five, collectively—who I can tell everything to. There's Jennifer [Stone], my friend Ashley, and Taylor [Swift] and my two cousins."

**Woo-Hoo**
Taylor Swift is Sel's love guru!

**On getting ready for a big event . . .** "I usually like to start getting ready two hours before because I like to take my time. I don't like scrambling. Normally I'll start with my hair, then I'll get up and play music and eat. I like eating before I get into my dress—it's more comfortable, plus I don't want to get food on my dress *before* I even start the night! And then right before

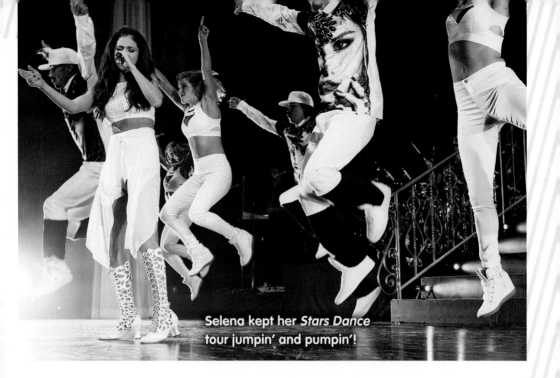

Selena kept her *Stars Dance* tour jumpin' and pumpin'!

I leave the house, I always look at my mom and say, 'How do I look?' I know she'll say something like 'Oh that's beautiful!' or 'That's my favorite thing you've ever worn!' And it always makes me feel confident—that way, I get to start the night thinking, YES!"

## On her eating and workout routines . . . "I eat junk. I'm from the South, so I love Mexican food, greasy pasta, and fried things. I do try, every now and then, to put something in my body that will be good, but honestly, I've never liked working out. I need to be active in some way, though—that's why I kind of secretly do it for my show. We have thirteen choreographed pieces, and it's a 90-minute set. I consider that my workout!"

Selena models one of her outfits for a Dream Out Loud fashion campaign.

**On her fashion sense . . .** "I [usually don't care] what I look like, I don't. I wish I could pay attention because Gwen Stefani, say, [always] looks flawless. Of course, when I'm on red carpets, I'm nervous, sweaty and weird."

**On a secret confession . . .** "[I have] headphones that I didn't mean to take from a photo shoot. They were a prop, and when I grabbed my stuff, I took them with me. They work pretty well! I still use them."

**On girl power . . .** "I love my girl friends more than I've loved any of my boyfriends, because they have supported me, loved me, and always stood by my side. Some girls will drop you in five seconds for the right guy. That's not how it's supposed to be. That's why I love Demi [Lovato] and Taylor [Swift]—they support females and love to have that empowerment—through fashion, best friends, and boys, boys, boys! My wish is that girls would love girls more."

**On Taylor Swift urging her to move to NYC . . .** "I honestly would love to go out there for a little while. I just don't know when. ...It's gonna be a minute, but I love New York."

"I WANT TO CHANGE THE WORLD ... I HAVE DREAMS!"

Selena really wakes up the crowd at *Good Morning America*'s Central Park concert.

# THE REAL SELENA SCRAPBOOK

## CHECK OUT THE STAR'S FRIENDS, FOOD, AND FUN FACTS

DREAM COSTAR? "IT WOULD BE A ROMANCE WITH ZAC EFRON! BUT THAT PROBABLY WON'T BE HAPPENING. I'M KIDDING! I'M KIDDING!"

# FASHION PASSION

### GO-TO OUTFIT
"Skinny jeans, a tank top, a scarf. That's my uniform for anything from the airport to a meeting."

### SNEAKERS
"I'm a high-top person!"

### BACK-TO-SCHOOL OUTFIT
"Good tights, a boyfriend-fit cardigan or sweater, cute tank tops, scarves—lots of layers!"

### PERSONAL STYLE
"I like trying new things . . . I don't think you should ever have to 'define your style.'"

### COMFORT CLOTHES
Flannel shirts

**2010**
Selena introduces Dream Out Loud fashion line.

# SELENA & FRIENDS

**Selena on Cody Simpson:** "Happiest of birthdays to bubba and such an incredible person. Love you inside out @codysimpson –here's to more"—Selena Instagrammed her buddy Cody Simpson on his 18th b-day.

**Selena on Taylor Swift:** "Every single problem I ever have is healable by Taylor Swift! If I ever have an issue, Taylor has gone through it, because she's older than me, and she gives the most thought-out answers. . . Because of her, I haven't lost faith. We literally talk every day."

**Selena on Katy Perry:** "I actually talked to her about guys who are intimidated by strong girls. I haven't found someone yet who could understand my lifestyle, support it, love me through it, and not be threatened by it."

**Bridgit Mendler on Selena:** Recalling the 2013 MTV Movie Awards, Bridgit described hanging out with Selena. "Basically, she's just a girl hanging out backstage before the show. She's so cool and chill. We actually had fun that time. That night we went to this haunted play. It was really cool."

**Demi Lovato on Selena:** "We've been through a lot together," Demi explained of her longtime friendship with Selena. "We've had periods of times when we grew apart, and we just didn't really talk. But now we're in a place where I think we realize that life is so short, and that when you have people in your life that love you so much, then you should just always be around them."

**Taylor Swift on Selena:** "I've known Selena through some of the most important years of both of our lives. I've seen her grow up gracefully and gradually in spite of all the pressure on her. Selena has learned to make and follow her own rules, when to take a chance on projects that are out of her comfort zone and when to walk away when something isn't right."

# FOODIE FINDS

SNACKS: Pickles, Texas popcorn (popcorn drizzled with hot sauce and dipped in pickle juice)

FOOD: Mexican

FLAVOR: Chocolate

DRINK: Pickle juice

FRUIT: Mango

PIZZA: Topped with jalapeños and mushrooms

ICE CREAM: Rocky road or chocolate

CANDY: Snickers, M&Ms, Kit Kat bars

THANKSGIVING DISH: Stuffing

THING TO BAKE: Cheesecake

CELEBRITY CHEF-MATE: Bridgit Mendler—
"[We] made chicken potpies from scratch.
They took a long time,
but they were so yummy."

GUILTY PLEASURE: McDonald's

INSTANT MEAL: Ramen noodles

# SELENA'S CHILL PLAYLIST

**"GOODBYE YELLOW BRICK ROAD"**
ELTON JOHN

**"HERE COMES THE SUN"**
THE BEATLES

**"LONGER"**
DAN FOGELBERG

**"VINCENT"**
DON MCLEAN

## Downloads
Sel loves to listen to all kinds of music.

# CHILDHOOD MEMORY

When Selena was in elementary school back in Texas, she had an experience she will never forget. "I was playing a crayon in a play. This boy backstage really liked me, had a big crush on me and I didn't like him. He was like, 'No, I like you! I like you!' and he kissed me and I pushed him on the stage. I was so mad and I ran off and I'm this crayon and I'm like storming off! It was awful but it was really cute!"

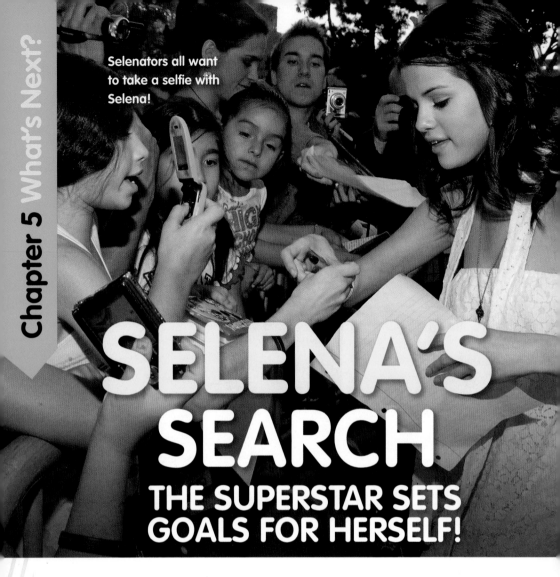

Selenators all want to take a selfie with Selena!

# SELENA'S SEARCH

## THE SUPERSTAR SETS GOALS FOR HERSELF!

"I don't feel like I can do enough for my fans," Selena told *Seventeen*. "I work a lot, I work hard, and I get tired. But when you walk onstage and see these people who wait *hours* outside just to see you, it's the greatest thing in the world. But it baffles me because they do so much for me and I don't feel like I can do enough for them."

Well, if you ask Selena's fans, they will all tell you that she has actually given them quite a bit! Her talent as a singer and actress has made them smile, laugh, and cry. They know that Selena has tried to be a role model for them, and she often shares her experiences (both good and bad) with them in the hope that it might help their decision making. She has shared her belief that we all should help others, and she has encouraged her fans to have a global charitable view so they can make a difference for the better.

Yes, Selena has gone through some huge transitions. She went from being a Disney child

> "I REALLY LIKE MAKING MUSIC TO MAKE PEOPLE DANCE."

actress to a teen idol to a young woman. During that time, she had to adjust her acting and singing style to fit her growing audience. She saw her personal life—whether it was her relationship with Justin Bieber or the birth of her baby sister, Gracie—covered in the tabloids and photographed by the **paparazzi**. In the meantime, she was also making some very grown-up decisions. She started her own production company, July Moon. She created fashion and perfume lines. She starred in more mature films, and she even moved out of her parents' home and bought her own mansion.

The spotlight has been very hard on Selena. At her

core, she is a very private person. But even though it can be tough having every move you make blasted in the headlines, Selena has been able to handle the pressure thanks to her inner circle. She has turned to them in the good times and especially in the bad times. "I've had those moments," she told *Teen Vogue.* "I think everybody has those moments, and it's good to have people around you who call you out on your [mistakes], because that's exactly what every single person in my life does on a daily basis. I like to say I have a good sense of judgment, but I know that not everybody does. The older I've gotten, the more I've learned that I have to open myself to all opportunities."

"FOR SOME REASON, EVER SINCE I TURNED 18, IT'S GOTTEN HARDER."

Selena has also been willing to let her fans see her growing pains. In October 2014, Selena stopped by *The Ellen DeGeneres Show.* Ellen asked her how she would grade herself from 1 to 10 on the improvements she has made in her life. "I'm a seven," Selena told her. "People tend to forget. They're like, 'Be yourself, be yourself,' and I'm still trying to figure out who that is. . . . So I just try to be the best I can be."

If the past is any indication of the future, Selena's best will bring her to amazing heights. Her hard work and

Selena enjoys a day at Malibu Beach! Surf, sand, and sun are her favorites.

dedication have led to a fan base that reaches from 8-year-olds to 30-year-olds. She has opened herself to new challenges and has learned quite a bit along the way. As for what drives her, Selena told TVGuide.com, "I don't plan, but there are goals that I'd like to achieve. I'd love to have a family one day; I'd love to move back to Texas . . . I'd love to win an Oscar."

But there's more in her heart and dreams, and it is very Selena! In an interview with *Flaunt* magazine, Selena confessed what she most wants the future to bring her: "I'm hoping I'm super satisfied with who I am."

# Resources

## BOOKS

Brooks, Riley. *Selena and Demi: Forever Friends*. New York: Scholastic, 2009.

Bernard, Jan. *Selena Gomez*. North Mankato, MN: The Child's World, 2012.

## ARTICLES

*Seventeen*, March 2014
"Selena Gomez: The Mogul"

*Billboard*, June 2011
"Selena Gomez: The *Billboard* Cover Story"

# Facts for Now

Visit this Scholastic Web site for more information on **Selena Gomez**
www.factsfornow.scholastic.com
Enter the keywords **Selena Gomez**

# Glossary

**audition** *(aw-DISH-uhn)* a short performance given to compete for a part in a play, film, or television show

**blocking** *(BLAH-king)* arranging the positions and movements of performers in film or stage productions

**cameo** *(KAM-ee-oh)* a small character part in a play or a movie, usually played by a famous actor or actress

**paparazzi** *(pahp-uh-ROT-zee)* photographers who snap pictures of celebrities when they are out in public

**pilots** *(PYE-luhts)* single episodes of a TV show that are used to determine whether an entire series should be produced

# Index

advice, 31
*Aftershock* movie, 23
American Music Awards, 23
auditions, 9, 10, 11–12
Austin, Jake T., 12, 14

*Barney & Friends* television
    show, 9–10, 18
Bieber, Justin, 43
birth, 6
books, 29
British *Cosmopolitan*
    magazine, 27

Canals-Barrera, Maria, 14
Cassidy, Katie, 21
charities, 26, 43
childhood, 6, 8–9, 27, 41
"Come & Get It" single, 21,
    22, 23
Cyrus, Miley, 12

Disney Channel, 11–12, 14, 19
Dream Out Loud fashion line,
    24–25, 37

education, 9, 10, 20, 26, 27, 41
Efron, Zac, 36
*Elle* magazine, 8, 9
*Ellen DeGeneres Show, The,*
    44
exercise, 33

Fact Files, 12–13, 14–15
fans, 20, 22, 26, 42, 43, 44, 45
fashion, 24, 25, 32–33, 34, 37
foods, 33, 40
fragrance, 25, 27
friendships, 10, 26–27, 32, 35,
    38–39

*Getaway* movie, 23
Gomez, Mandy (mother), 6, 8,
    9, 11, 33

Gomez, Ricardo (father), 6

*Hannah Montana* television
    show, 12
"Heart Wants What It Wants,
    The" single, 23, 24
heatworld.com, 11
Henrie, David, 12, 14
*High School Musical 3: Senior
    Year* movie, 19
home, 17, 35, 43
*Hotel Transylvania* movies, 23

*In Dubious Battle* movie, 23
"I Want to Know You" single, 31

journal, 29–30
July Moon company, 43

King, Joey, 20
*Kiss & Tell* album, 17, 19

*Lizzie McGuire* television show,
    12
Lovato, Demi, 10, 11, 12, 26,
    35, 39
"Love You Like a Love Song"
    single, 18

McCartney, Jesse, 15
Meester, Leighton, 21
Mendler, Bridgit, 39, 40
*Monte Carlo* movie, 20, 21–22
MTV Movie Awards, 39
*MTV News,* 24
*Muppets, The* movie, 23

"Naturally" single, 17
Neo fashion line, 25

paparazzi, 43
Perry, Katy, 38
playlist, 41

*Princess Protection Program*
    movie, 18
privacy, 44

*Ramona and Beezus* movie,
    19, 20–21
*Revised Fundamentals of
    Caregiving, The* movie, 23
"Round & Round" single, 17

Selena Gomez & the Scene
    band, 17–18, 19, 20, 23
*Seventeen* magazine, 18, 42
Simpson, Cody, 38
social media, 7
*Spy Kids 3-D: Game Over*
    movie, 10
*Stars Dance* album, 21, 23–24
*Stars Dance* tour, 22, 24
Stone, Emma, 26
Stone, Jennifer, 14, 32
*Suite Life of Zack & Cody, The*
    television show, 12
Swift, Taylor, 26, 27, 32, 35,
    38, 39

Teefey, Gracie (sister), 43
Teen Choice Awards, 18, 19,
    21, 22

*Walker, Texas Ranger: Trial by
    Fire* movie, 10
*When the Sun Goes Down*
    album, 17–18, 20
"Who Says" single, 17–18
*Wizards of Waverly Place*
    television show, 12, 14, 17
Woman of the Year award, 21

*Year Without Rain, A* album,
    17, 20
"Year Without Rain, A" single,
    17

# Acknowledgments

**Page 6:** Mom's support: perezhilton.com November 7, 2014
**Page 8:** Gas and concerts: *Elle* July 2012; Texas girl: *Emmy* magazine
**Page 9:** Entertain herself: *Emmy* magazine; *Barney* audition: *Elle* July 2012; Learning on *Barney*: people .com November 7, 2014
**Page 10:** Mean girls: *Tiger Beat* April 2010
**Page 11:** Disney search: *Time Out New York Kids* 2010; Disney audition: heatworld. com August 6, 2013; Remember where you came from: *Discovery Girls*
**Page 12:** Dream On burst: intotheglass.com October 2014
**Page 17:** *Wizards* last day: *Girls' Life* August/September 2011
**Page 18:** "Who Says": *Seventeen* March 2014

**Page 19:** *High School Musical 3: New York Daily News* 2008; Inspire blurb: We Day Speech March 27, 2014
**Page 20:** Littles: *Teen Vogue* June/July 2011; *Ramona & Beezus*: Scholastic Classroom Magazines April 29, 2010
**Page 22:** *Monte Carlo*: cinemanerdz.com July 4, 2012
**Page 24:** Writing songs: inquisitr.com November 23, 2014
**Page 25:** Dream Out Loud line: *MTV News* October 15, 2009; Neo line: capitalfm.com July 12, 2013
**Page 26:** We Day speech: Associated Press
**Page 27:** Friends: *Harper's Bazaar* April 2013; Taylor Swift: British *Cosmopolitan* October 2010; Fragrance: Press release
**Page 28:** Make people dance: *On Air with Ryan Seacrest* April 5, 2013

**Page 29:** Books: Scholastic interview July 11, 2010; Journal: Scholastic interview April 29, 2010
**Page 30:** Latina role model: *Elle* July 2012
**Page 31:** Performing advice: *First News* March 19, 2012
**Page 32:** Famous in Hollywood: *Glamour* September 2011; Besties: *Seventeen* 2012; Getting ready: *Seventeen* November 2010
**Page 33:** Workout: *Teen Vogue* December/January 2014
**Page 34:** Fashion sense: *Harper's Bazaar* April 2013; Secret confession: *People* July 29, 2013
**Page 35:** Girl power: *Seventeen* March 2014; Moving to NY: inquisitor.com November 24, 2014; Change the world: *Seventeen* March 2014

**Page 36:** Zac Efron: *Seventeen* March 2014
**Page 37:** Go-to outfit: *Teen Vogue* September 2014; Sneakers: *TeenVogue* September 2014; Back-to-school outfit: *Teen Vogue* September 2014; Personal style: *People* June 20, 2012
**Page 38:** Selena on Cody: Instagram January 13, 2015; Taylor Swift: *Seventeen* 2013; Katy Perry: *Seventeen* March 2014
**Page 39:** Bridgit Mendler: MTV Movie Awards 2013; Demi Lovato: heatworld.com May 17, 2013; Taylor Swift: *InStyle* June 2013
**Page 40:** Celeb chef-mate: *InStyle* June 2013
**Page 41:** Childhood memory: British *Cosmopolitan* 2010

# About the Author

Marie Morreale is the author of many official and unofficial celebrity biographies. She attended New York University as an English/creative writing major and began her writing and editorial career in New York City. As the editor of teen/music magazines *Teen Machine* and *Jam!*, she covered TV, film, and music personalities and interviewed superstars such as Michael Jackson, Britney Spears, and Justin Timberlake/*NSYNC. Morreale was also an editor/writer at Little Golden Books.

Today, she is the executive editor, Media, of Scholastic Classroom Magazines writing about pop-culture, sports, news, and special events. Morreale lives in New York City and is entertained daily by her two Maine coon cats, Cher and Sullivan.